CHRONOLOGICAL LIST
OF MEN AND EVENTS

	IN ITALY	IN OTHER COUNTRIES		
1300	Dante (w)			
			Gunpowder	
			The Black Death	
	Petrarch (w)	Wiclif (r.w.)	The 100 Years War	
	Boccaccio (w)	Chaucer (w)		
		Huss (r)		
1400				1400
	Brunelleschi (a)			
		The van Eycks (p)	Cosimo de' Medici	
	Ficino (ph)	Roger v. d. Weyden (p)	Joan of Arc	
		Fouquet (p)	Printing	
		Memlinc (p)	Fall of Constantinople	
		van der Goes (p)		
	Politian (w)	Villon (w)	Louis XI	
	Lorenzo de' Medici (w)		Lorenzo de' Medici	
	Savonarola (r)	Schongauer (e.p.)		
	Leonardo da Vinci (s)	Bosch (p)	Discovery of America	
1500	Bramante (a)	Dürer (p)	French in Italy	1500
	Ariosto (w)	Luther (r)	Reformation	
	Machiavelli (ph)	Calvin (r)	Spaniards in Italy	
	Loyola (r)	Copernicus (s)	Charles V, Emperor	
	Michelangelo (a.w.)	Holbein (p)	Henry VIII	
		Rabelais (w)	Philip II	
	Tasso (w)	Bruegel (p)	Elizabeth	
	Palladio (a)	Montaigne (w)	Lepanto	
	Palestrina (m)	Cervantes (w)	The Armada	
	Bruno (r)	Shakespeare (w)		
1600	Monteverde (m)	El Greco (p)	Henri IV	1600
		Rubens (p)		
	Galileo (s)	Rembrandt (p.e.)	North America colonized	
		Descartes (s)	Thirty Years War	
		Velasquez (p)	Richelieu	
	Bernini (a)	Milton (w)	Cromwell	
	Borromini (a)	Poussin (p)		
		Molière (w)		
		Wren (a)	Louis XIV	
	Stradivarius	Newton (s)		
1700	D. Scarlatti (m)	Watteau (p)		1700
	Vivaldi (m)	Handel (m)	Peter the Great	
	Vico (ph)	Bach (m)	Marlborough	
	Goldoni (w)	Voltaire (ph)		
	Piranesi (e)	Rousseau (ph)	Frederick the Great	
		Haydn (m)	England takes	
		Kant (ph)	India, Canada	
		Mozart (m)	American Revolution	
		Goya (p)	French Revolution	

Architects (a), engravers (e), musicians (m), philosophers (ph), religious leaders (r), scientists (s), writers (w), painters (p). Italian painters and sculptors on opposite page.

page 4   (*Acknowledgments*): These works of art, which the Museum of Modern Art is exhibiting on their way back to Italy, were originally lent by the Royal Italian Government for exhibition at the Golden Gate International Exposition in San Francisco. Although the New York exhibition was arranged through negotiations opened directly with the Museum by the Italian representatives, the Museum is of course greatly indebted to the authorities of the San Francisco Exposition, through whose efforts the Italian works of art were first brought to this country, and particularly to the courageous initiative and diplomatic skill of *Dr. Rudolph Heinemann*, Director of the Thyssen Museum, Lugano, the European Envoy to the Golden Gate International Exposition at San Francisco, and *Dr. Walter Heil*, Director of the M. H. de Young Memorial Museum, San Francisco, Chairman of the Department of Fine Arts at the San Francisco Exposition.

Professor Clarence Kennedy of Smith College designed and supervised the sculpture lighting, volunteering his services; to assist him *Mrs. Kennedy* and *Mr. H. L. Logan* of the Holophane Company generously gave their time.

Professor Cesare Brandi, as well as *Comm. Ventura*, was of great assistance in advising upon the installation of the exhibition.

Color plates

The color plates, as is usually the case with the inexpensive four-color process, are inaccurate and vary considerably within a single printing. The following notes indicate some of the principal faults.

cover   (Fra Angelico color plate): blues and greens too pale; reds satisfactory. The vertical shadows at left and right were caused by unavoidable frame shadows when the color separations were photographed.

ftsp.   (Botticelli color plate): sky too bright; hair too violet; flesh tones too pink.

page 8   (Bellini color plate): too bluish over all; drapery of John the Baptist should be olive rather than violet green. The lower margin with the signature has been cut off.

page 10   (Palma color plate): colors too cold and bright; greens should be yellowish rather than bluish.

page 12   (Parmigianino color plate): green of background too blue; flesh tones too ruddy.

page 13   (Gentileschi color plate): blues and yellows have lost their purity; the blue is too violet, the yellow too red; the background and veil are too green.

Other corrections

page 14   It is possible that this bust was done *after* Donatello's return from Padua to Florence about 1453 rather than before his departure for Padua in 1443. (The relation between the medallion and Cosimo de' Medici's cameo makes implausible Bode's placing of the bust in the sculptor's Paduan decade and his identifying the subject with Antonio da Narni.)

pages   While Verrocchio's *David* was sold by the Medici in 1476, it may have been
22, 23   commissioned and executed at any time during the previous four or five years.

page 29   (Botticelli): *add* Washington (National Gallery) *to list of museums*.

page 34   The reproduction of the *Madonna of the Chair* has been turned slightly toward the left: the post of the chair should be *vertical*.

page 37   (Bronzino): *add* Ottawa *to list of museums*.

page 62   *For* the rise and fall of Napoleon *read* the rise and decline of Napoleon.

The lists of American museums owning works attributed to artists represented in the exhibition were of necessity assembled in great haste: they are neither critical nor complete but err principally by including too many paintings of questionable attribution.

Italian Masters

BOTTICELLI : Detail from *The Birth of Venus*

SEE PAGE 26

Italian

Masters

LENT BY THE ROYAL

ITALIAN GOVERNMENT

January to March, 1940

NEW YORK

THE MUSEUM OF MODERN ART

Contents and Index of Artists

Preface

Botticelli's *Birth of Venus*, Titian's *Paul III*, a Michelangelo marble (the first ever exhibited in New York), Raphael's *Madonna of the Chair*, Verrocchio's *David*, Bernini's *Costanza Buonarelli*, Masaccio's *Crucifixion:* that these should be brought together in a single exhibition is a memorable event, but that this exhibition should be in New York is an unexpected miracle.

What art museum would not be glad to assist in this miracle? For these world famous masterpieces can and should claim the hospitality even of a museum devoted to the art of our day. Actually this is not the first time the Museum of Modern Art has shown the art of the past: African Negro art, some of it as old as the 15th century, Aztec and Mayan art of five to ten centuries ago, and even the 20,000-year-old cave paintings of paleolithic man have been shown in the museum. These exhibitions were pertinent because the works of art in them have been appreciated only in recent years and also because modern artists have been among the pioneers in this new appreciation. But these primitive or exotic arts, stimulating as they are, are merely tangential to our culture; they do not really belong to it. In fact, even if we should combine the influence of all these exotic traditions upon modern art, we would find the total far less important than the influence of the art represented in this exhibition.

For the Renaissance and Baroque art of Italy stands at the very heart of the great tradition of European art and its American branches — the tradition* which looks back to Greece and forward through El Greco, Poussin, Rubens, Rembrandt to Ingres, Delacroix, Manet, Renoir and then to masters of our own days as widely separated as Picasso and

*See chart inside back cover.

Diego Rivera. Cézanne above all recognized this when he said he wanted to paint "something solid and enduring like the art of the museums," which meant to him the art of the great Venetians and Florentines and their French descendants. Beside these masters, the value of the Ivory Coast mask, or, say, the Japanese print to the modern artist, must ever be superficial and transitory.

The Exhibition of Italian Masters was not, of course, planned as a complete survey of the field, but considering that only twenty-eight works are included, it does give some idea both of the scope and the quality of the periods† represented.

The Early Renaissance, 1400-1500. There were very great medieval artists in Italy during the hundred and fifty years before the earliest work in our exhibition: Giotto, for instance, and the Sienese masters. Our exhibition begins, however, with the first and in many ways the greatest master of the early Renaissance, Donatello. It was Donatello who fused in his sculpture the new enthusiasm for the ancient art of Greece and Rome with the new understanding of form, movement and space, based both upon the sciences of anatomy and perspective and upon new habits of exact observation. This new realism was first given dignity and power in painting by Masaccio whose great frescoes inspired even Raphael and Michelangelo two generations later. (pages 14, 19.)

Donatello's researches were further carried on by his followers Pollaiuolo and Verrocchio, in Florence, and Mantegna in the north. The aristocratic and somewhat reactionary side of Florentine painting at the end of the early Renaissance is magnificently represented by Botticelli's *Birth of Venus*, which is,

†See chart inside front cover.

6

however, a little off the main highway in its sophisticated estheticism. In Northern Italy, the early Renaissance is well shown in the paintings of Mantegna, already mentioned, and Giovanni Bellini, leader of the Venetian School. (pages 21, 23, 26, 38, 42.)

Although it is easy to tell the story of Italian Renaissance painting in terms of scientific or realistic advances, it is essential to remember that these technical innovations were in themselves of no artistic consequence. They did however offer new and exciting possibilities to those artists who were great enough to give artistic *form* to the new discoveries.

The High Renaissance and Mannerism, 1500-1600.

This mastery of the art of form is most clearly and authoritatively revealed in the brief period of the High Renaissance. The charming, adolescent awkwardness of the 15th century, its minor moods and discoveries, its delightful but distracting details, are put aside. A new sense of dignity, maturity and grandeur takes their place. The idealized human figures, their forms and movements, the colors of their draperies, are grandly and simply composed in paintings devoid of all technical, esthetic or psychological trivialities. Very few works of art ever perfectly fulfilled these lofty ideals except in a negative way. But the Grand Style of the High Renaissance is well represented in our exhibition by Michelangelo's marble relief, Raphael's *Madonna of the Chair*, the Palma Vecchio, and Titian's *Paul III*; less importantly by the Sebastiano del Piombo (pages 33, 35, 36, 42, 47).

Almost before the High Renaissance had come to maturity about 1510 it lost its classic balance and disintegrated into the variety of styles and states-of-mind now called Mannerism. Michelangelo's power and Raphael's grace were exaggerated first by the masters themselves and then by their followers. Mannerism brought with it affectation, distortion, expressionism and at the same time a more personal and modern approach to painting, a new spirit well illustrated by the portraits of Lotto and Parmigianino. Tintoretto's *Miracle of St. Augustine* with its deep space and dramatic lighting carries us past Mannerism almost to the Baroque. (pages 44, 45, 48.)

The Baroque, 1600-1750.

A violent reaction against Mannerism and against an eclectic attempt to revive the Grand Style took place in Rome under the revolutionary leadership of Caravaggio, who more than any single artist created the dominant movement in Baroque art of the 17th century. Caravaggio's shocking realism, extravagant emotionalism, melodramatic handling of light, contempt for "good taste" and apparent disrespect for tradition overwhelmed Italian art and spread throughout Europe. Bernini with even richer technical and imaginative gifts held a position of equal importance in Baroque sculpture. The Italian Baroque continued well past the middle of the 18th century and produced many artists whose importance is only beginning to be appreciated in this country. Those who chose the exhibition are to be congratulated upon the number of Baroque works included; among these are two masterpieces, the Bernini bust and Cavallino's *St. Cecilia.* (pages 53, 57, 59.)

Two pages are scarcely enough for even an elementary layman's preface to such an exhibition. But paintings and marbles and bronzes such as these will triumph over any inadequacy of introduction.

Welcome, then, to these great works of art—and after we have enjoyed them may they return safely to the land which gave them life.

ALFRED H. BARR, JR.

Director, The Museum of Modern Art

SEE PAGE 42

GIOVANNI BELLINI: *Madonna with St. Catherine and John the Baptist*

SEE PAGE 42

PALMA VECCHIO: *Holy Family with St. Catherine and John the Baptist*

11

PARMIGIANINO: *Portrait of a Lady*

SEE PAGE 45

GENTILESCHI: *Virgin and Child*

SEE PAGE 54

1 DONATELLO: *Bust of a Young Man*

Bronze; height, 16½ inches; made about 1440. Sometimes called *Portrait of Antonio da Narni.* Lent by the National Museum (Bargello), Florence.

Donatello was not only the foremost Italian sculptor before Michelangelo but also, more than any other single figure, the founder of Renaissance art. He was born about 1386 and worked for a time with Ghiberti, the last of the great Florentine Gothic sculptors. In 1402, while still a boy, he went with the architect Brunelleschi to Rome to dig among the ruins for ancient sculpture — a momentous expedition for it marks, as well as any one event, the beginning of the Renaissance, the rebirth of a widespread enthusiasm for the art of Greece and Rome. Donatello was, however, not an imitator of ancient sculpture. He was primarily a great realist who tempered and disciplined his art by a respect for classical form. His realism was no mere surface imitation of natural forms but the result of a profound study of the anatomy and structure of the body. He was also deeply interested in the esthetics both of ideal beauty and of expressive, shocking ugliness.

In his long career Donatello passed through almost as bewildering a variety of styles as Picasso. By the time of his death in 1466, his influence had been diffused throughout Italy. In Florence a dozen excellent sculptors were his followers, among them Pollaiuolo (page 20) and Verrocchio (page 22). Painters too came under his sway not only in Florence but in the North where Mantegna (page 38) who had studied Donatello's sculpture in Padua spread his influence far and wide through Venice and Lombardy and even into Germany.

The *Bust of a Young Man* was done about 1440, midway in Donatello's career. Its spare strength and aristocratic grace are informed with a greater classicism of style than is usual in Donatello's sculpture. No one knows who the young man was but the medallion is an enlarged copy of an antique cameo owned, at the time the bust was made, by Cosimo de' Medici whose court was the center of the new neoplatonic cult. The bust, with its medallion which suggests a platonic symbol of the soul, may indeed have been inspired by a passage in Plato's *Phaedrus.** Neoplatonism appears again in Botticelli's *Birth of Venus* (page 26) painted for another Medici some fifty years later.

---

*See R. Wittkower, "A Symbol of Platonic Love in a Portrait Bust of Donatello," in the *Journal of the Warburg Institute*, vol. I, Jan. 1938, p. 260-61.

15 • DONATELLO

Detail, a little over half original size.

2 FRA ANGELICO: *The Naming of John the Baptist*

Panel, 10¼ x 9-7/16 inches. Painted about 1430. Lent by the Royal Museum of San Marco, Florence.

" . . . the angel said unto him . . . thy wife Elizabeth shall bear thee a son and thou shalt call his name John . . . . And Zacharias said unto the angel, Whereby shall I know this? for I am an old man and my wife well stricken in years . . . And the angel answering said . . . Behold, thou shalt be silent and not able to speak until the day that these things shall come to pass, because thou believedst not my words . . .

"Now Elizabeth's time was fulfilled . . . and she brought forth a son. And her neighbors and kinsfolk . . . rejoiced with her . . . and they made signs to his father, what he would have him called. And he asked for a writing tablet, and wrote, saying, His name is John."

(From the Gospel of Luke, Chapter 1.)

See color plate on cover.

This panel, like the Masaccio *Crucifixion* on the following page, is a transitional work linking late medieval or Gothic painting with the new art of the Early Renaissance. Gothic are the gay flower-garden colors, the graceful trailing robes, the doll-like tiny-handed figures, but from the new scientific realism of the Renaissance comes the scientific perspective (demonstrated a little ostentatiously in the corridor at the right), the out-of-door atmosphere and the realistic modeling of the head of Zacharias which suggests that the painter had seen, though only half understood, the epoch-making frescoes which the great pioneer Masaccio had painted in the Brancacci Chapel from 1426 to 1428.

The Naming of John the Baptist comes from Fra Angelico's own convent of San Marco. Some critics suggest that the panel may not be by the master's own hand but by that of a studio assistant.

Fra Angelico (Giovanni da Fiesole) was born in 1387 and at the age of twenty became a Dominican monk. From 1436 to 1443 he was at work on the famous series of frescoes in the cells and public rooms of the convent of San Marco at Florence which was under the patronage of Cosimo de' Medici. Later he went to Rome to paint murals in the Vatican at the invitation of the Pope. He became prior of San Marco and died in 1455 having, according to Vasari, refused the archbishopric of Florence. He has been beatified.

At his best Fra Angelico was a master of grandly simple composition and of lyrical effects of light and color. Above all he was, in a time of growing paganism, secular vanity and scientific scepticism, a Christian artist, pious, childlike and devout. There are paintings by Fra Angelico in the museums of Boston, Cambridge (Fogg), New York (Metropolitan) and Philadelphia.

3 MASACCIO: *The Crucifixion*

Panel, 33½ x 25½ inches. Painted in 1426. Lent by the Royal Gallery, Naples.

To the left of the cross is the Virgin with hands clasped; to the right St. John looks down in meditative sorrow; between them Mary Magdalen kneels in a vermilion robe, her arms flung high in despair. These attitudes and gestures, these gradations of grief accentuated by different intensities of color, the general symmetry of the composition, the gold background and the Gothic arched frame are traditional elements which Masaccio inherited. But to this medieval heritage Masaccio added new scientific techniques which were being studied by some of his older contemporaries such as Donatello, the sculptor. The convincing anatomy of the Christ's torso, the striking foreshortening of the figure seen from below with the head sunk between the shoulders, the powerful modeling of the forms in light and shade, the carefully studied realism of the Magdalen's drapery are all technical achievements of a new scientific period. Masaccio's importance, however, lay not so much in his mastery of new techniques but in his ability to create with these new methods works of art of a gravity, seriousness and dramatic power which made him the greatest Italian painter of his generation and the central link of the great tradition which passed from Giotto a century before to Michelangelo a century later.

The Crucifixion was originally the topmost panel of a large altarpiece commissioned on February 19, 1426 for the Church of the Carmine in Pisa. The high position of the panel explains the foreshortening of Christ's body as if seen from below. The surface has suffered some damage and the St. John has been partly repainted.

Masaccio (Tommaso di ser Giovanni di Simone Guidi) was born near Florence in 1401. At the age

Detail, about two-fifths original size.

of twenty-six he was already engaged in his greatest work, the series of frescoes in the Brancacci Chapel, Florence — frescoes which were to be studied by subsequent generations of Florentine painters. By 1429 he was dead, having won for himself in a few brief years a place among the greatest masters.

4 POLLAIUOLO: *Hercules and Antaeus*

Bronze; height, 17¾ inches. Made about 1460 (?) Lent by the National Museum (Bargello), Florence.

According to the legend, Hercules meets in combat the demigod Antaeus, who derives fresh strength each time he touches the earth, his mother.

To overcome him, Hercules lifts Antaeus high in the air and crushes out his life. Antaeus flings back his head in one last gasping, terrible shout. The two bodies, each bent back like a strung bow, are bound together by the terrific tension of Hercules' grip so that their radiating limbs form a centrifugal design.

The extraordinary violence and brutality of this small bronze are characteristic of Pollaiuolo who carried on, as a specialist, the study of the body in active movement which had been only one of Donatello's many interests. Vasari, some fifty years after Pollaiuolo's death, wrote of him, "He skinned many bodies in order to see the anatomy beneath and he was the first to show how to study the muscles which give form and organization to figures." The *Hercules and Antaeus* is proof that he could embody his researches in superb esthetic form. The modeling is, in fact, so powerful and simple that only the ornamental tortoises beneath the triangular base remind one that Pollaiuolo was also a goldsmith. The *Hercules and Antaeus* is probably related to several large paintings of the Hercules legend which Pollaiuolo did for Lorenzo de' Medici about 1460.

Pollaiuolo (Antonio di Jacopo Benci) was born in Florence in 1429 and died in Rome in 1498. Besides working as a painter and sculptor, he was the first great Italian engraver. There are paintings by him in the museums of Boston (Gardner) and New Haven (Yale) and sculpture in New York (Frick), Detroit and Washington (National).

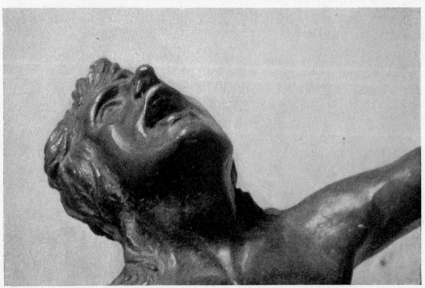

Detail, approximately original size.

21 • POLLAIUOLO

5 VERROCCHIO: *David*

Bronze; height, 48 inches. Made in 1476. Lent by the National Museum (Bargello), Florence.

This figure of the youthful David is one of the most beloved and famous works of 15th century Italian sculpture. The awkward grace of the body, the subtly ambiguous expression of the face, the fastidious realism of the whole figure are characteristic of Verrocchio's art at this period.

Andrea Verrocchio was born in Florence in 1435. Like Pollaiuolo, he was a follower of Donatello. His art reached its climax in the heroic equestrian figure of Colleoni in Venice on which he was working when he died in 1488. Verrocchio was also a painter and among his pupils was Leonardo da Vinci who was probably still in his studio at the time the *David* was cast. Verrocchio is represented in the museums of New York (Metropolitan) and Washington (National).

Detail, about half original size.

The *David* was commissioned by Lorenzo and Giuliano de' Medici in 1476 and sold by them in the same year to the Florentine government. We reproduce a photograph of the back of the figure because the head of Goliath which was cast separately and then fixed to the base obscures the line of the leg and interferes with an appreciation of the beauty of the pose.

23 • VERROCCHIO

6 LAURANA: *Portrait of a Lady, possibly Eleonora of Aragon*

Marble; height, 17 inches. Made about 1470. Lent by the National Museum, Palermo.

The sculptor has emphasized the underlying globelike form of the head by using sleek, continuous surfaces which he breaks just as little as possible by the sharply chiseled edges of the eyebrows, nostrils and lips. The light coming through these sharp edges accentuates the translucent quality of the marble, and the smoothness of the marble flesh is contrasted with the delicately rendered textures of the gown and close-fitting cap. The baffling simplicity of the technique reinforces the enigmatic charm of the face.

Francesco Laurana, sculptor, architect and medalist, was born about 1420 and worked in Naples, in Sicily, where this bust was done, and in Southern France, where he died shortly after 1500. He was comparatively isolated from the main currents of Italian art and developed his own original and personal style which is best seen in his long series of portrait busts of women. There is sculpture by Laurana in the museums of New York (Metropolitan, Frick) and Washington (National).

25 • LAURANA

See color detail, frontispiece.

7 BOTTICELLI: *The Birth of Venus*

Tempera on linen, 66¾ x 108¼ inches. Painted about 1485-1490. Lent by the Royal Uffizi Gallery, Florence.

"One saw

Born in the sea, free and joyous in her acts,
A damsel with divine visage
Driven ashore by the ardent zephyrs
Balancing on a shell; and it seemed the heavens rejoiced thereat.

. . . .

You could swear that you could see the goddess coming from the waves
Wringing out her hair with her right hand
And with the left covering the sweet mount of desire,
And the sand, once trodden by her feet,
Clothing itself with grass and flowers.
Then with joyous and expectant glance
You would have seen her clasped by the three nymphs
And wrapped in a starry robe."*

It is very probable that these verses of Politian, celebrating the great Medici festival of 1475, guided Botticelli in painting his *Birth of Venus*. The painter has changed certain details and has turned the poet's gay mood to one of subtle sadness.

Botticelli was the foremost painter and Politian the favorite poet at the court of Lorenzo and Giuliano de'

Medici, where enthusiasm for Greek culture and neo-platonic philosophy had become almost a religion. Older Florentine artists, Donatello and Pollaiuolo, had admired classical sculpture for its formal perfection or its mastery of anatomy and movement but in the Medicean circle and especially in Botticelli's painting the passion for the ancient world was colored by a delicate sentimentality, a mood of esthetic revery. This mood is reflected in *The Birth of Venus* in the sweet poignancy of the goddess' face and even in the sad eyes of the puffing winds.

The style of *The Birth of Venus* is as dematerialized and otherworldly as its sentiment. The standing figures seem almost as weightless as the winds. The intricate curving lines of drapery and hair, the dancing accents of the waves, the pale colors touched with gold highlights combine to make a supreme masterpiece of decoration as well as of poetry.

The Birth of Venus was painted about 1485-1490 as a decoration for the country house of a cousin of Lorenzo the Magnificent. It was a companion piece to the equally famous *Primavera* or *Spring* painted somewhat earlier. The pose of the Venus was influenced by classic figures of the *Venus de'* Medici type, but her face is traditionally supposed to be that of the beautiful mistress of Giuliano de' Medici, Simonetta, whose untimely death in 1476 was mourned by Medicean poets.

*From the *Stanze per la Giostra*, 1476-78. The translation is given in *A History of Italian Painting* by Frank Jewett Mather, Jr., New York, 1923, p. 255. Politian was in turn inspired by a Greek Hymn to Aphrodite.

Detail, a little over one-third original size.

Botticelli (Alessandro di Mariano Filipepi) was born in Florence in 1444-45. He studied with Fra Filippo Lippi but was greatly influenced by Pollaiuolo and Verrocchio. In the 1480's he painted frescoes for the Pope in the Sistine Chapel, and illustrated Dante for the same patron for whom he painted *The Birth of Venus*. His poetic melancholy turned to deep religious fervor under the influence of the fanatical reformer, Savonarola, who preached against the paganism of the Medici. His late, comparatively abstract style is torn by a tragic expressionism. He died in 1510, neglected in the midst of the High Renaissance.

In the middle of the 19th century his art was "rediscovered" by such writers as Ruskin and Walter Pater until he became one of the cult figures of late 19th century estheticism. His place now seems secure among the great Italian masters just short of the first rank. There are paintings by Botticelli in the museums of Boston (Gardner), Cambridge (Fogg), Chicago, Detroit, New York (Metropolitan), Philadelphia.

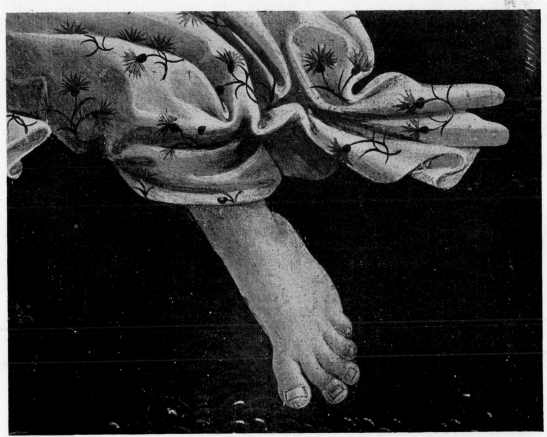

Detail, about one-third original size.

8 ANDREA DELLA ROBBIA: *The Annunciation*

Glazed terra cotta; Virgin, 65 inches high; Angel, 62 inches high. Lent by a Private Collector.

For over a century the della Robbia family specialized in relief sculpture done in glazed terra cotta, an inexpensive substitute for marble. Luca della Robbia, one of the great Florentine sculptors of the mid-15th century, perfected the technique and created the style which was carried on into the 16th century by an active studio headed by his nephew, Andrea della Robbia, who was born in 1435 and died in 1525. Andrea's finest pieces, while preserving much of the charm and nobility of his uncle's art, are touched with a certain wistful melancholy. His most famous works are the series of round reliefs of white figures of babies against blue backgrounds which he made for the Foundling Hospital of Florence.

In this group of the Annunciation, God the Father and the dove symbolizing the Holy Ghost appear above the Virgin Mary and the angel Gabriel. Each of the four pieces was cast separately. The group comes from the Oratorio delle Anime del Purgatorio, a chapel near the Church of San Niccolò, Florence. It appears to be identical with the one mentioned by Bocchi-Cinelli in *Le Bellezze della Città di Firenze*, 1677 (p. 281), as being in the Palazzo Tempi. There is sculpture by Andrea della Robbia in the museums of Boston, Detroit, New York (Metropolitan) and Philadelphia.

9 MICHELANGELO: *Madonna and Child*

Marble bas-relief (circular); diameter, 38¼ inches. Executed about 1504. Lent by the National Museum (Bargello), Florence.

This relief of the Madonna is an early work of the greatest Italian sculptor, but already, at the age of twenty-nine, Michelangelo's art was mature enough to imply something of the grandeur of his later style.

Within the marble circle the sculptor has composed the figures of the Mother and Child roughly in the form of a pyramid. Instead of softly rounding the forms as Raphael was to do in his *Madonna of the Chair*, Michelangelo emphasizes the sharp angles of the seated body, the elbow, and the knee, surrounding them by the curves of the drapery and the Child's body.

The Mother holds an open book before the Child who rests His elbow upon it without seeming to read. She herself looks away with an air of detachment and noble melancholy which again is in marked contrast to the somewhat complacent spirit of Raphael's picture. Behind her stands the young John the Baptist.

Vasari, a younger contemporary of Michelangelo, writes that this relief was done in 1504 for Bartolommeo Pitti of Florence. It was left unfinished but the marks of the chisel which can be seen over much of the surface give a variety of texture which adds to the esthetic quality of the sculpture — at least so far as modern eyes are concerned.

Michelangelo Buonarroti was born at Caprese of Florentine parents in 1475. He first studied painting with Ghirlandaio and learned much from Masaccio's frescoes in the Brancacci Chapel. Then, before 1490, he began to study sculpture with Bertoldo, an aged pupil of Donatello, in the school for sculptors established by Lorenzo de' Medici. There he came in contact with neoplatonic philosophy which, together with the poetry of Dante and the contemporary preaching of Savonarola, colored his thought during the rest of his life. During the Savonarola revolution he fled to Bologna for a brief time. Between 1496 and 1501 he lived in Rome and then returned to Florence. His two most important early sculptures are the *Virgin with the Dead Christ on her Knees*, now in St. Peter's, and the gigantic *David*, both done before the relief in our exhibition.

Early in 1505, Michelangelo went to Rome to work on the tomb of Julius II, the first of a series of colossal undertakings among which may be mentioned the ceiling frescoes and the *Last Judgment* in the Sistine Chapel, the Medici tombs in San Lorenzo in Florence, the Laurentian Library of the Medici, the group of buildings on the Capitoline in Rome and the transformation of St. Peter's.

He died in 1564 at the age of almost ninety years. In the course of his long and troubled life he had changed the character of the arts of painting, sculpture and architecture.

33 • MICHELANGELO

10 RAPHAEL: *Madonna of the Chair*

Circular panel, 28 inches in diameter. Painted about 1512. Lent by the Royal Pitti Gallery, Florence.

The *Madonna of the Chair* is possibly Raphael's most loved work and one of the most generally admired paintings in the world. It rivals in popular affection even Corot's *Dance of the Nymphs,* van Gogh's *Sunflowers* and, in America, Whistler's *Mother.*

In Raphael's other most renowned painting, the *Sistine Madonna,* the Virgin is seen standing among clouds as a heavenly queen adored by saints. But in the *Madonna of the Chair* she is presented as a comely matron with kerchief and shawl seated with her child held comfortably in her arms. In this way, by making holiness charming and divinity familiar, Raphael has transformed a sacred mystery into an agreeable domestic tableau.

The *Madonna of the Chair* presents a skilful and gracious solution of the difficult problem of composing a group of figures within a circle. The circle and the soft curves within it are stabilized by the strong verticals of the chair and the back of the Madonna. The color is obscured somewhat by the yellowness of aging varnish.

Nothing is known of the early history of the *Madonna of the Chair* though in the Museum at Lille there is a preliminary drawing on the same sheet of paper as a study for the circular *Alba Madonna* formerly in the Hermitage Museum, Leningrad, and now in the National Gallery of Art at Washington as a part of the Mellon bequest. It is interesting to compare both in sentiment and in composition the *Madonna of the Chair* with Michelangelo's circular *Madonna* in marble done seven or eight years before (page 33).

Raphael (Raffaello Sanzio *or* Santi) was born at Urbino in the Apennines in 1483. He studied with Perugino and later, in Florence, during the years 1500 to 1508, came under the influence of Leonardo da Vinci. In 1508 he was called to Rome by Pope Julius II. In the Vatican he painted his greatest works, the large frescoes of the *Stanze* or antechambers which surpass in importance his numerous Madonnas and his few but superb portraits. Raphael's late work suffered from an effort to emulate the art of his titanic rival, Michelangelo. He died in Rome in 1520 at the age of thirty-seven.

Raphael's influence on his contemporaries and followers was immense, and during succeeding centuries his lucid, orderly and calculated art has been at the very core of the academic tradition. Many great artists have acknowledged his mastery, Poussin and Ingres, for instance, and, less directly, Degas, Renoir and, in our own day, Picasso.

Paintings by Raphael are in the museums of Baltimore, Boston (Gardner), New York (Metropolitan, Bache), Washington (National).

35 • RAPHAEL

11 SEBASTIANO DEL PIOMBO: *Portrait of a Lady, called "La Fornarina"*

Oil on canvas; 26¾ x 21⅝ inches. Dated 1512. Lent by the Royal Uffizi Gallery, Florence.

The voluminous forms and rich color give evidence of Sebastiano's Venetian training but the firm, smooth modeling of the figure suggests the influence of his Roman colleague Raphael. The picture was in fact for many years thought to be a portrait by Raphael himself of his mistress, La Fornarina.

Sebastiano del Piombo (Sebastiano Luciani) was born in Venice in 1485 and studied the art of Giorgione. About 1510 he went to Rome where he became a close friend of Michelangelo. He died in 1547. There are paintings by him in the museums of New York (Metropolitan, Historical Society), Philadelphia and Sarasota (Ringling).

12 BRONZINO: *Portrait of a Lady*

Panel; 42⅞ x 33½ inches. Painted about 1540. Lent by the Royal Gallery, Turin.

The stiff formal pose, the stolid *hauteur* of the lady, the metallic modeling of the flesh, the emphasis upon the magnificent silks and damasks and jewels of her costume are characteristic of the Florentine portraits of the mid-16th century which set the style for pompous official portraits all over Europe. The acid gold and crimson against the beautifully painted gray- and brown-striped curtain give the painting distinction.

Some critics suggest that the painter of this portrait is Pontormo, the master of Bronzino, but the repainted condition of parts of the picture makes accurate attribution difficult.

Agnolo Bronzino was born in Florence in 1502 and worked for many years with Pontormo who had been a pupil of Andrea del Sarto. Bronzino was court painter to the Grand Dukes of Florence and was a superb technician within the limits of his icy, enamel-like style. He died in 1572. There are paintings by him in the museums of Boston (Gardner), Chicago (Art Institute), New York (Metropolitan, Frick) and Worcester.

13 MANTEGNA: *St. George*

Panel, 26 x 12⅝ inches. Painted about 1462. Lent by the Royal Gallery of the Academy, Venice.

The saint stands quietly looking toward the setting sun. Behind him stretches a minute landscape with a road winding up to a walled town on a hill. The painted frame which surrounds him like a doorway is interrupted by the dragon's snout, the broken lance and the cord from which hangs a garland of fruit. Everything is painted with metallic miniature detail which, however, does not seriously diminish the sparkling clarity of the composition, the emphatic relief of the figure, or spacious effect of distance; nor does it obscure the contemplative and curiously untriumphant mood of the saint. The *St. George* was painted in Mantua about 1462 when the artist was in his early thirties.

Andrea Mantegna was born near Vicenza in 1431. He studied at Padua with the archeologically-minded Squarcione and the best of the Venetian Gothic painters, Jacopo Bellini, whose daughter he married. He was also profoundly influenced by the great Florentine sculptor Donatello who had spent a whole decade in Padua during Mantegna's youth (see page 14).

Thus three of the principal forces at work in mid-fifteenth century Italian painting — the rediscovery of classical art, the Gothic love of detailed realism, and the scientific researches in anatomy and perspective of the Florentines — were absorbed by Mantegna who not only mastered them completely, but made further important explorations of his own. His intelligence, science, integrity and mastery of form made him a guide to a whole numerous generation of North Italian artists of whom the greatest was his brother-in-law, Giovanni Bellini (page 42). Mantegna spent most of his mature life in Mantua and died there in 1506. Paintings by him are in the museums of Boston (Gardner) and New York.

Detail, about five-sixths original size.

39 • MANTEGNA

14 LUINI:

The Body of St. Catherine Borne by Angels to Sinai

Fresco transferred to canvas, 47⅝ x 102¼ inches. Lent by the Royal Brera Gallery, Milan.

This charming and cleverly composed decoration is one of a series of frescoes painted between 1520 and 1525 by Luini and his pupils for the Pelucchi family at Monza near Milan. It is the only fresco in the exhibition: *fresco* means, literally, "fresh" and refers to the method, used by most Italian mural painters, of painting with powdered colors and water on fresh plaster.

Bernardino Luini, most famous of Milanese painters, was born at Luino near Lake Maggiore about 1475 and died in Milan 1531-32. The style of his work was dominated by that of Leonardo da Vinci who worked in Milan during Luini's youth. There are paintings by Luini in the museums of Boston, Cambridge (Fogg), Cleveland, Detroit, Minneapolis, New York, Philadelphia, Sarasota (Ringling) and Washington (National).

Detail.

15 CORREGGIO: *Madonna and Child*

Panel, 22¾ x 17⅝ inches. Painted about 1515. Lent by the Royal Estense Gallery, Modena.

Soft tints, soft forms and contours, a graceful pose, gentle, almost sugary sentiment — these obvious qualities may lead one to overlook the subtlety of the color harmony with its accents of yellow and green against pale blue and violet and the perfection of the composition in which the vertical formed by the mother's torso is reinforced by the child's arms and then cut by the transverse parallels of the child's body and the mother's arm and head.

Antonio Allegri da Correggio was born about 1494 near Modena, but painted most of his life in Parma where he died in 1534. He was influenced at first by Mantegna and Leonardo and later by Raphael and Michelangelo. His greatest work was the astounding dome fresco of the Cathedral of Parma which anticipated by a century the Baroque church decorators. He and his follower Parmigianino (page 45) were also among the chief pioneers of Mannerism, the fashionable style of the mid-16th century. There are paintings by Correggio in the museums of Detroit and Philadelphia.

16 BELLINI: Madonna with St. Catherine and John the Baptist

Panel, 21⅝ x 30¼ inches. Signed IOANNES BELLINUS. Painted 1510-1520. Lent by the Royal Gallery of the Academy, Venice.

See color plate, page 8

The two saints balance each other on either side of the Madonna but a slight shifting of her figure, the diagonal position of the Child, and the elaborately contrasted saints save the painting from a too formal symmetry. The mood of quiet contemplation, each figure absorbed in his own thoughts, is characteristic of the late work of Bellini after he had come somewhat under the influence of his pupil Giorgione. Behind the figures stretches a landscape bathed in a golden light with a seaport and hills dotted with castles and, beyond these, pale mountains reaching to the sky.

For stylistic reasons some critics think this painting was done either by Andrea Previtale or another good assistant of Bellini.

Giovanni Bellini was born in Venice about 1430, the son of the painter Jacopo Bellini who was also Mantegna's teacher. Mantegna (see page 38) in turn greatly influenced the young Giovanni. For

17 PALMA VECCHIO: Holy Family with St. Catherine and John the Baptist

Oil on canvas 49½ x 76¾ inches. Painted 1520-1530. Lent by the Royal Gallery of the Academy, Venice.

See color plate, page 10

Although it is possible that they were done in the same decade, Palma's magnificent painting belongs to the High Renaissance, while Bellini's altarpiece opposite looks back to the 15th century. The Bellini is simple and symmetrical in composition, Palma's boldly asymmetric; Bellini's color is comparatively light and clear, Palma's sumptuously rich; Bellini's Madonna is girlish, timid, Palma's mature and confident; Bellini's saints are isolated and raptly introspective, Palma's engaged in a courteous conversation. In Palma's composition the Grand Style is in full flower.

As is the case with several important Venetian paintings of this period, the authorship is not entirely certain. Some critics feel sure that Titian himself painted the superb figure of St. Catherine as well as the romantic landscape; the Madonna is also very close to that in Titian's great altarpiece of the Pesaro family.

Jacopo Palma, il Vecchio (the elder), was born near Bergamo

thirty years of his long life he was the foremost master of Venice, yielding place in his last decade to his two great pupils, Giorgione and Titian. He died in 1516, having founded through his serene and gracious art the Venetian school of painting. The following American museums own paintings by Giovanni Bellini: Baltimore (Walters), Boston (Gardner), Cambridge (Fogg), Chicago, Detroit, New York (Metropolitan, Bache, Frick, Morgan), Ottawa, Philadelphia, San Marino (Huntington), Washington (National).

Detail of landscape background almost two-thirds original size.

about 1480 and died in Venice in 1528. About 1505 he was working in Giovanni Bellini's studio. For a brief time after Giorgione's death in 1510 he was Titian's chief competitor for the leadership of the Venetian school. There are paintings by him in the museums of Cambridge (Fogg), Chicago, Detroit, Philadelphia, Sarasota (Ringling), Worcester.

Detail of landscape background about one-fourth original size. This part of the canvas is thought by several authorities to have been painted by Titian rather than by Palma.

18 LOTTO:

Portrait of a Young Man

Oil on canvas, 13¾ x 11 inches. Painted about 1525. Lent by the Municipal Museum of the Sforza Castle, Milan.

In the midst of the confident, grandiose formality of Venetian life and art of 1525, Lotto's portraits strike a surprising note of intimacy. About this young man, for instance, there is an air of modesty and shy uncertainty. The composition and color are as subtle as the characterization. The youth leans forward tentatively, the black-striped violet gray of his jacket contrasted against the bottle green of the background. The sharp shadow on the forehead curiously continues the shape of the cap. The whole is beautifully painted, especially the hands and collar.

Lorenzo Lotto was born probably in Venice about 1480 in the same generation as Giorgione, Palma and Titian, but he left the metropolis early and worked in the provinces, living a retiring and pious life. He died in 1556. In spirit his art is more related to Mannerism than to the persistent High Renaissance character of his Venetian contemporaries. There are paintings by him in the museums of Cambridge (Fogg), Detroit, New York (Metropolitan), Philadelphia and Washington.

19 PARMIGIANINO:

Portrait of a Lady

Oil on canvas, 55 x 33⅝ inches. Painted about 1525 or 1535. Lent by the Royal Gallery, Naples.

See color plate, page 12.

In a period when Michelangelo, Titian and Correggio were in their prime an artist even of Parmigianino's talent must be given a secondary place. Yet this painting of a girl is one of the most beautiful portraits of the 16th century in its simple pose, arrestingly direct expression and rich color. The fine drawing of head and hand suggests the contemporary Holbein or even the much later Ingres. Its great distinction can be appreciated by comparing it with the somewhat earlier *"Fornarina"* of Sebastiano del Piombo (page 36) or Bronzino's later *Portrait of a Lady* (page 37).

The *Portrait of a Lady* was traditionally supposed to represent the famous Roman courtesan Anthea, mentioned by Pietro Aretino and Benvenuto Cellini, but in view of the lady's appearance and indicated character this seems improbable. More likely she was a daughter of the aristocratic Sanvitale family of Fontanellato near Parma. The standing pose cut off at the knees was Parmigianino's invention.

Parmigianino (Francesco Mazzola) was born in Parma in 1503 and died there in 1540. He was influenced by Correggio, then by Raphael. The slender and affectedly elegant figure style in his religious paintings places him among the pioneers of Mannerism, the dominant art movement of the mid-16th century. He was a brilliant portraitist and the first important Italian etcher. There is a painting by him in the Detroit Institute of Art.

20 TITIAN: *Portrait of Pope Paul III*

Oil on canvas, 41¾ x 32¼ inches. Painted in 1543. Lent by the National Museum, Naples.

Titian's *Paul III* is one of the great portraits of the world both as a penetrating characterization and a superb painting. Titian's psychological acuteness in his handling of the face, the eyes, the hands is so explicit that descriptive words are superfluous. A yellow varnish has somewhat dulled the richness of the color but one may call attention to the magical brushwork of the white sleeve and the red velvet chair arm. This painting is one of a magnificent series of portraits of the Farnese family by Titian now in the Naples Museum.

Titian (Tiziano Vecelli), the greatest of Venetian painters, was born about 1477 at Pieve di Cadore, north of Venice. He worked in Giovanni Bellini's studio and later assisted Giorgione whose influence he felt during his early years. He used at first a comparatively firm, tight technique but in his later work the brush stroke became broad and rapid. The *Paul III* comes in the middle of his career when his technique was already fairly loose and transparent. Titian died in 1576, painting great pictures to the very last of his ninety-nine years. There are paintings by him in the museums of Baltimore, Boston (Gardner), Detroit, Kansas City, Minneapolis, New Haven (Yale), New York (Metropolitan, Frick, Bache), Philadelphia, St. Louis and Washington (National).

21 TINTORETTO: *St. Augustine Healing the Plague-Stricken*

Oil on canvas, 102¾ x 68¾ inches. Lent by the Municipal Museum, Vicenza.

This painting is above all a demonstration of Tintoretto's extraordinary mastery of complex dynamic composition — a faculty which was developed in a more abstract form by his follower El Greco and has been greatly admired in modern times by Delacroix, Cézanne and many of our own contemporaries.

Tintoretto conceives his picture as an interplay of forces which thrust against one another to form an equilibrium. Though the canvas is of course a flat surface, the artist by means of modeling in light and shade, perspective, foreshortening and overlapping planes has made his composition seem powerfully three-dimensional. The natural forms used by the artist to embody his pictorial forces are for the most part human bodies which lean or bend or gesture as active units in a dynamic symphony.

The first note of the symphony is struck by the powerful figure of the man in the left foreground whose leaning torso sets in motion a strong diagonal thrust which is taken up both by the dark ascending line of the hill at the right and (in depth) by the two figures, one behind the other, in the middle distance. This major diagonal is crossed by a minor one indicated by the more distant sloping hill at the left. The general sense of activity is reinforced throughout by the rippling outlines of bodies and hills. Ultimately the whole intricate composition of contours and solids, lights and darks, thrust and counterthrust recedes into the background and comes to rest on the quiet lines of the distant church, the door of which is almost exactly in the center of the canvas.

The *Saint Augustine* is probably from the late period of the master and was done as an altarpiece for the church of San Michele in Vicenza. The blues are now surely much brighter in relation to the other colors than they were when the picture was new.

Tintoretto (Jacopo Robusti) formed with Titian and Veronese the great Venetian trio whose careers spanned the major part of the 16th century. He was born in Venice in 1518 and died there in 1594. On the walls of his studio he wrote the words, "The drawing of Michelangelo and the color of Titian." To this magnificent formula he applied the fire of his own impetuous and romantic genius — so much so, indeed, that his art shocked his contemporaries (including Titian) by its tumultuous, overwhelming violence. There are paintings by Tintoretto in the museums of Baltimore (Walters), Boston (Fine Arts, Gardner), Cambridge (Fogg), Chicago, Cleveland, Detroit, Hartford, Minneapolis, Montreal, New York (Metropolitan, Morgan), Ottawa, Philadelphia, St. Louis.

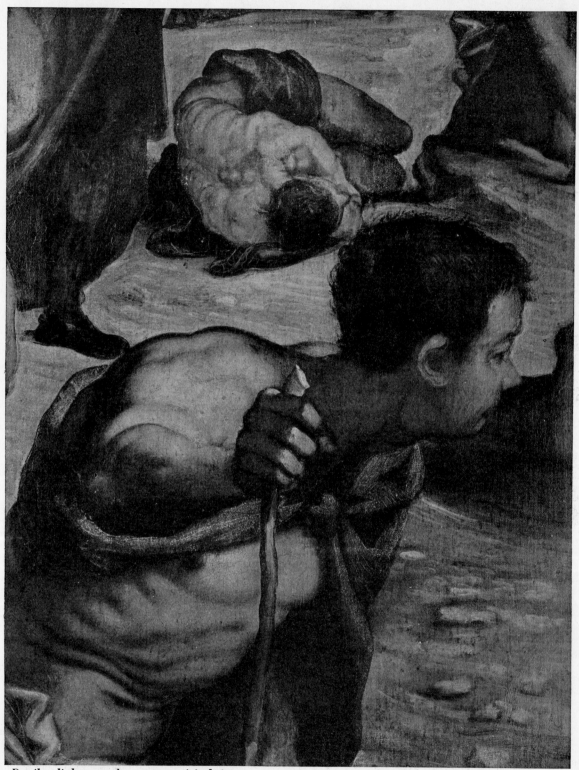

Detail, a little more than quarter original size.

Detail, a little over half original size.

22 CARAVAGGIO: *Boy Bitten by a Lizard*

Oil on canvas, 25¼ x 20 inches. Painted about 1590. Lent by Professor Roberto Longhi, Rome.

"He also painted a boy who is bitten by a lizard darting out from among flowers and fruit; and it looked as if that head really was screaming, and the whole was carefully finished."* Thus wrote Caravaggio's biographer (and rival) of a picture which was lost for many years but is plausibly the recently discovered painting in our exhibition. In any case, the sensational incident, the vivid realism both of surface detail and of action, the coarse face of the boy, the theatrical lighting and, just as much, the breadth and vigor of the forms, are all characteristic of Caravaggio's art.

Caravaggio (Michelangelo Merisi) was at once the most influential and the most revolutionary artist of his time and, if we except the youthful Rubens and the recluse, El Greco, he can also be called the greatest. He was born in Caravaggio, near Milan, in 1573. Before 1590 he had arrived in Rome where his early works such as the *Boy Bitten by a Lizard*, painted before he was twenty years old, show already his defiant rejection both of the dying Mannerist tradition and of the new academic reform movement founded by the Caracci. "He simply copied those forms which appeared to his eyes," an outraged critic complained. In other words, he seemed to be throwing overboard the great intellectual, classical, idealistic tradition of Italian art as it had come down from Giotto through Masaccio and Leonardo to Raphael, Michelangelo and Titian. He even committed the sacrilege of ignoring ancient art. Taken to see two famous antique statues he was unimpressed. " 'See how many masters nature has provided for me and other artists,' he said, pointing to some bystanders, 'without your statues.' And he called a gypsy girl and, taking her to his lodgings, painted her in the act of telling a young man his fortune...."†

Actually, like most great revolutionaries in art from Donatello to Cézanne and Picasso, Caravaggio had a deeper understanding of the great traditions than the academic nonentities who attacked him. Some of his greatest works were also among the soundest classic compositions of his time. But it was his shocking innovations which gathered the young artists to his banner. Many of them were excited by his novel interest in commonplace or low-life subject-matter, or by his radical interpretation of traditional themes; others were influenced by his melodramatic lighting, or by his contempt for academic authority, and generally hardboiled attitude both in life and in art.

Before he died in 1610 he had begun to dominate the art of Italy, and in the succeeding generation his style overwhelmed Europe. Ribera, Velasquez, Zurbarán, Murillo; Poussin (in his early work), de la Tour, and the Le Nains; Rubens, Hals, Rembrandt, Vermeer and dozens of lesser Northerners all came more or less under his influence; and through the Spaniards his realistic attitude descended to Courbet, Manet and their hundreds of 19th century followers throughout Europe and America. Paintings by, or very close to, Caravaggio are to be found in the museums of Hartford, Cambridge (Fogg), Chicago, Kansas City and Princeton.

*From G. Baglioni *Vite de' Pittori*, Rome, 1642, cited by T. Borenius in "An Early Caravaggio Re-discovered," *Apollo*, July, 1925.
†From Bellori's *Vite de' Pittori Moderni*, Rome, 1672, quoted by Arthur McComb in *The Baroque Painters of Italy*, Cambridge, Mass., 1934, p. 35.

53 • CARAVAGGIO

23 GENTILESCHI:
Virgin and Child

Oil on canvas, 39⅜ x 33½ inches. Painted about 1620. Lent by Count Alessandro Contini-Bonacossi, Florence.

Though Gentileschi is called the foremost Roman follower of Caravaggio, he was actually an independent spirit who took the bright enameled color and brilliant rendering of draperies such as may be seen in the Florentine Mannerist painting of Bronzino (page 37) and added to these something of Caravaggio's early work without, however, following that master in his violent light effects. Gentileschi's harmonies of gold and blue, his luminous shadows and beautiful surfaces have suggested to some critics a comparison with Vermeer of Delft.

Orazio Gentileschi was born in Pisa about 1565, grew up in Florence, and was working at the end of the century in Rome at the time when Caravaggio was leading his revolution. He was called to London by Charles I about 1625 and died there about 1647. His daughter Artemisia was the best woman painter in the history of Italian art.

See color plate, page 13.

24 GUERCINO:
Bath of Diana

Oil on canvas, 12½ x 20½ inches. Painted about 1615. Lent by the Gallery of the Carrara Academy, Bergamo.

Following the conventional landscape formula of the period, the rich warm tones of the foreground grow cooler as they recede until they become cold blue green in the misty distance. This orderly recession is accented by the charming and simply modeled figures in the foreground and the bright orange tree in the middle distance.

Landscape painting was considered among the Italians an inferior kind of art during most of the period covered by this exhibition. There are fine landscapes in the Mantegna (page 38), the Bellini (page 42), and the Palma (page 42) but these are primarily backgrounds for figures. About 1600 in Italy painting landscapes began to be more respectable, but important and successful artists such as Guercino still felt it better to paint figures in the foreground so that the picture could be called *The Bath of Diana* (even adding in the distance a tiny Actaeon torn by his dogs).

Guercino (Giovanni Francesco Barbieri) was born in 1591 and died in 1666. He studied at the Academy of the brothers Caracci at Bologna but soon after, in Rome, came under the influence of Caravaggio. Though he and other members of the Caracci school painted great altarpieces and decorations, they also developed Italian landscape painting to the point where it was taken up by the great Frenchmen living in Rome, Poussin and Claude Lorrain. There are paintings by Guercino in the Baltimore (Walters), Detroit, Minneapolis and Providence museums.

Detail, about three-fifths original size.

25 CAVALLINO: *St. Cecilia*

Oil on canvas, 24 x 19¼ inches. Painted about 1645. Lent by the National Museum, Naples.

The blind Cecilia, patron saint of music, leaving her violin on the floor, kneels in ecstasy as the angel holds a crown above her head. This is a small picture but one with such extraordinary grandeur of scale that it grows in the memory to many times its actual size. Its contrasting tones of yellow and blue were often used in an obvious manner by earlier painters such as Gentileschi (page 13) and Bronzino (page 37); but Cavallino muffles them in Caravaggesque lighting until the colors seem to glow like dust-encrusted jewels. The *St. Cecilia* is perhaps Cavallino's best work; for sumptuous quality of painting it ranks high among the masterpieces of Italian Baroque art.

Passing through Naples in 1607 Caravaggio inspired a whole school of excellent artists among whom, in the second generation, Bernardo Cavallino was the most distinguished. Cavallino was born in 1622 and died in 1654. There are paintings by Cavallino in the museums of Boston, Hartford and Kansas City.

Detail, about three-fifths original size.

57 • CAVALLINO

26 BERNINI: *Portrait of Costanza Buonarelli*

Marble; height 28⅜ inches. Made about 1625. Lent by the National Museum (Bargello), Florence.

In this vivid, pulsating portrait of his mistress may be felt something of the electric vitality and passion of the extraordinary artist who made it. In one way, however, the *Portrait of Costanza Buonarelli* is exceptional in Bernini's art for it is an intimate and personal work by an artist most of whose commissions were public and official: fountains, churches, tombs and portraits of popes, kings and cardinals.

Gian Lorenzo Bernini was born in Naples in 1598. At an early age he came to Rome where he was trained in sculpture by his father and studied intensively Roman marbles and the work of Michelangelo. He became the supreme European sculptor of the 17th century and held that position until his death in 1680 at the age of eighty-two. He was also a painter, a designer for the theater, a brilliant draughtsman and one of the greatest architects of his time as the colonnade of St. Peter's bears witness.

Bernini's sculpture was the result of extraordinary technical virtuosity, emotional intensity, vaulting imagination and a reckless disregard of artistic propriety. He set out "to mould the marble like wax" and to "fuse to some extent sculpture and painting." In his early *Apollo and Daphne*, for instance, he carved in marble a whole branch with leaves, and later, in the main apse of St. Peter's, he made a sunburst of sculptured sun-

beams, angels and flamboyant clouds. The *Costanza Buonarelli* is equally but less obviously skilful in its sensitively rendered hair, parted lips and eyes with subtly differentiated pupils.

So overwhelming was the influence of Bernini that, as Panofsky has said, the sculpture of the High Baroque might as well be called the Berninesque. His reputation today is rapidly recovering from a period just coming to a close when technical virtuosity and realism, however vital, were too commonly despised.

There are terra cottas attributed to him in the Fogg Museum at Cambridge.

59 • BERNINI

27 TIEPOLO: *A Council of the Knights of Malta*

Oil on canvas, 49¼ x 76⅜ inches. Lent by the Municipal Museum, Udine.

In 1748 two noblemen of Udine, a town north of Venice, appeared before the Grand Council of the Knights of Malta to obtain the admission to the Order of the noble families of their town. One of them, Count Montegnacco, commissioned Tiepolo to paint the scene, giving him an exact description of the reception which had taken place in the great council chamber of the palace of the Grand Master.

Tiepolo met this difficult problem brilliantly, characterizing each figure with remarkable inventiveness and giving an eye-witness vividness of detail to an event which he had never seen. The ceremonial blacks of the knights' robes are relieved by discreet foreground accents of gold, blue and scarlet and the whole is held together by the rose tone of the background wall. Though this is not a characteristic work of Tiepolo it falls into the great Venetian tradition of pageant painting which goes back to Gentile Bellini and Carpaccio three hundred years before.

Giovanni Battista Tiepolo, born in Venice in 1696, was the last important Italian master of the Baroque period and one of the greatest decorative painters of all time. Basing his art to a large degree on that of Veronese, he painted numerous large decorations in and near Venice, in Würzburg and in Madrid

Detail, from foreground, one half original size.

where his works influenced the youthful Goya. He died in Spain in 1770. There are paintings by him in the museums of Baltimore (Walters), Boston (Fine Arts, Gardner), Chicago, Cleveland, Detroit, Hartford, Kansas City, Minneapolis, New Haven (Yale), New York, Philadelphia, Princeton, Springfield, Toledo, Washington (National).

61 • TIEPOLO

28 ALESSANDRO LONGHI: *Portrait of Giulio Contarini*

Oil on canvas, 40⅛ x 36 inches. Painted about 1765. Lent by the Gallery of the Concordi Academy, Rovigo.

This portrait of a shrewd and aging Venetian, the gray hair of his wig falling upon the pale gray fur and watery blue of his gown, brings the exhibition to a close on a minor key. This is perhaps appropriate since the painter, Alessandro Longhi, was the last distinguished Italian artist of the great tradition which perished toward the end of the 18th century in a paralysis of neoclassic academism.

Longhi was born in 1733 and studied with his more famous father, Pietro. He was one of the best portraitists of his time and painted such brilliant contemporaries as Cimarosa, Tiepolo, and Goldoni. He lived to an old age, saw the rise and fall of Napoleon, and died in 1813, ten years after the extinction of the Venetian Republic.

There are paintings by Longhi in the museums at Boston (Gardner) and New York (Metropolitan).

63 • LONGHI

Introductory Reading List

Among books in English, the general reader will find several introductions to Italian Renaissance art, notably: Heinrich Wölfflin, *The Art of the Italian Renaissance* (New York, Putnam, 1928); Bernhard Berenson, *The Italian Painters of the Renaissance* (Oxford, Clarendon Press, 1930); Frank Jewett Mather, Jr., *A History of Italian Painting* (New York, Holt, 1923).

For social and cultural backgrounds there is Jacob Burckhardt, *The Civilization of the Renaissance in Italy* (English translation reprinted by Phaidon Press, 1937). The most important early source of information is Giorgio Vasari, *Lives of the Most Eminent Painters, Sculptors and Architects* (first published 1550, English translation conveniently reprinted in 4 vols. by Everyman's Library).

The most modern and profusely illustrated general history in English is Raimond van Marle, *The Development of the Italian Schools of Painting* (19 vols., The Hague, Nijhoff, 1923-38). Valuable lists and indexes are contained in Bernhard Berenson, *Italian Pictures of the Renaissance* (Oxford, Clarendon Press, 1932).

Much less has been published in English on later Italian art. There is no readily available discussion of Mannerism, and but little has appeared on Baroque art. However these books will prove helpful: Arthur McComb, *The Baroque Painters of Italy* (Harvard University Press, 1934); Timon Henricus Fokker, *Roman Baroque Art* (2 vols., Oxford University Press, 1938); Giuseppe Fiocco, *Venetian Painting of the Seicento and Settecento* (Florence, Pantheon Press, 1929).

In addition to general treatises, there are many monographs on individual artists. The majority will be found listed in the above-mentioned books. Recently a number of excellently illustrated books at moderate prices have appeared on the following artists: Michelangelo (3 vols., Editions Tel; 2 vols., Phaidon Press); Botticelli (Phaidon Press); Titian (Phaidon Press); Tintoretto (Phaidon Press).

FORTY THOUSAND COPIES OF THIS BOOK HAVE BEEN PRINTED FOR THE TRUSTEES OF THE MUSEUM OF MODERN ART IN JANUARY 1940, BY WILLIAM E. RUDGE'S SONS, NEW YORK.